The Healing Power of Forgiveness

by Holly Roberts Merrell

Illustrations by Galih Winduadi

The Healing Power of Forgiveness

Copyright © 2019 by Holly Roberts Merrell
Illustrations: Galih Winduadi

All rights reserved. No part of this book may be reproduced by any mechanical, photographic, or electronic process, or in the form of a phonographic recording; nor may it be stored in a retrieval system, transmitted, or otherwise be copied for public or private use-- other than for "fair use" as brief quotations embodied in articles and reviews without prior written permission of the publisher. The intent of the author is only to offer information of a general nature to help you in your quest for emotional and spiritual well-being. In the event you use any of the information in this book for yourself, the author assumes no responsibility for your actions.

Library of Congress Control Number: 2020902155

ISBN: 978-1-951982-08-9
Digital ISBN: 978-1-951982-09-6

Buddha once said that "holding on to anger is like grasping a hot coal with the intent of throwing it at someone else; You are the one who gets burned".

Did you know that our negative emotions such as anger, hate, jealousy, shame, blame, and many others are like hot coals? If we hold onto them, we are going to get burned. These emotions can cause all sorts of problems in our bodies. They can cause our head to hurt and our back to ache. They can cause us to have allergies. They can even cause cancer and diabetes. For me, that anger, hurt and blaming caused red bumps on my face. It also caused a disease that doctors say is incurable. But can I tell you something, my illness is GONE!

You see, our bodies are designed to heal themselves. But when we have all of these negative emotions, they get in the way, and our bodies don't heal properly. So I gave up all these emotions, which I didn't even realize I had. I guess I had buried them deep down inside me. But when I finally admitted to these emotions and forgave and let them go, I finally healed! I no longer have any of the aches and pains that I used to. How cool is that? I am healthy and pain-free. And do you know what? That's the way it's supposed to be! We don't have to live with all those aches and pains and problems. And for me, the key was to simply forgive and let go of all that garbage buried within me. Maybe it will work for you, too. Its worth a shot.

So read through this book and think of those people who may have hurt you, and choose to forgive and let it go. And remember, the hardest person to forgive is usually ourselves. We can do some pretty dumb things sometimes, but hey, that's life. We're here to learn and grow.
So learn from it, move on, forgive yourself and let go.

You are worth it! You deserve it!

I forgive my mother,
I forgive my dad.
I forgive myself
for the rough times I've had.

I forgive my brother
and my sister, too.
I forgive everybody
for the dumb things they do.

I forgive myself
for making a mistake.
It's just part of life
for goodness sake.

Don't hold onto it,
just let it go.
Learn from what happened
and next time say no.

I forgive myself
for doing something wrong.
I choose to let it go.
I choose to stay strong.

Life's about learning,
from our ups and our downs.
We do silly things,
and we make funny sounds.

But laugh at yourself,
don't be too hard on you.
Forgive yourself
for those crazy things you do.

Repeat to yourself,
these words through the day,
and again at night
as you kneel down to pray.

I forgive, I forgive, I forgive!

I forgive you,
and I forgive me.
I can decide
who I want to be.

I don't have to hold on
anymore to this hate.
I'm letting it go,
before it's too late.

I'm freeing myself ,
from this hurt and this pain.
I'm freeing myself,
from this ball and this chain.

When I hold on to anger
it just weighs me down.
It pulls at my smile
until it's a frown.

So choose to forgive,
and let it all go.
Say these words again,
and just let them flow.

I forgive, I forgive, I forgive!

The more you do this
you'll begin to see,
the anger will fade,
and you will be free.

You may not have anger
that you need to let go,
but you can still say these words,
and your countenance will glow.

Sometimes it's buried
and we're not even aware
that there's some anger or hurt
hiding deep down in there.

So say these words daily
even though it seems strange.
Forgive every day,
and you'll see a change.

Now the best time to do this
is at night before sleep.
Close your eyes and relax,
now these words you'll repeat.

I forgive, I forgive, I forgive!

When we're more relaxed
with not a lot going on,
is when our bodies heal best,
from dusk till dawn.

So as you lay there each night
relaxed in your bed,
say these words over
and over in your head.

I forgive, I forgive, I forgive!

Don't say them just once,
but time and again.
Not even five times,
but better yet ten.

How about twenty
or thirty and some,
over and over
till your mind becomes numb.

The more that you say them
the more they'll sink in.
And you'll begin to awake
each morning with a grin.

You will feel happier,
you will feel more free.
You will feel healthier
like you're meant to be.

Remember these words,
repeat them each day.
"I now promise myself,
these words I will say…"

I forgive, I forgive, I forgive!

If you want to see results
a little bit faster,
these next words repeat
till you have them mastered.

They are very powerful
and heal just the same.
It can be fun saying them
if you make it a game.

You can say them fast
and you can say them slow.
You can say them high
and you can say them low.

You can say them with an accent.
You can say them with a drawl.
You can write them in a notebook.
You can write them on your wall.

Let's scratch that last one, your mom might get mad, and I don't want to receive any wrath from your dad.

So write it on paper
or repeat it in your head,
but do it quite often,
especially in bed.

As I said before,
our bodies heal best
each night as we lay down,
and our mind takes a rest.

So here are the words
that I want you to repeat.
Say them over and over
and negative emotions you'll defeat.

I RELEASE ALL ANGER,
I RELEASE ALL SHAME,
I RELEASE ALL BITTERNESS,
I RELEASE ALL BLAME!

Say them over and over,
again and again.
Not just once or twice
but more like five or ten.

I RELEASE ALL ANGER,
I RELEASE ALL SHAME,
I RELEASE ALL BITTERNESS,
I RELEASE ALL BLAME!

Now keep this up,
say these words every day,
and share what you've learned
to help others on their way.

I FORGIVE! I FORGIVE! I FORGIVE! I FORGIVE! I FORGIVE!
  I FORGIVE! I FORGIVE! I FORGIVE! I FORGIVE!
I FORGIVE! I FORGIVE! I FORGIVE! I FORGIVE! I FORGIVE!
  I FORGIVE! I FORGIVE! I FORGIVE! I FORGIVE!
I FORGIVE! I FORGIVE! I FORGIVE! I FORGIVE! I FORGIVE!
  I FORGIVE! I FORGIVE! I FORGIVE! I FORGIVE!
I FORGIVE! I FORGIVE! I FORGIVE! I FORGIVE! I FORGIVE!
  I FORGIVE! I FORGIVE! I FORGIVE! I FORGIVE!
I FORGIVE! I FORGIVE! I FORGIVE! I FORGIVE! I FORGIVE!
  I FORGIVE! I FORGIVE! I FORGIVE! I FORGIVE!
I FORGIVE! I FORGIVE! I FORGIVE! I FORGIVE! I FORGIVE!
  I FORGIVE! I FORGIVE! I FORGIVE! I FORGIVE!
I FORGIVE! I FORGIVE! I FORGIVE! I FORGIVE! I FORGIVE!
  I FORGIVE! I FORGIVE! I FORGIVE! I FORGIVE!
I FORGIVE! I FORGIVE! I FORGIVE! I FORGIVE! I FORGIVE!
  I FORGIVE! I FORGIVE! I FORGIVE! I FORGIVE!
I FORGIVE! I FORGIVE! I FORGIVE! I FORGIVE! I FORGIVE!
  I FORGIVE! I FORGIVE! I FORGIVE! I FORGIVE!
I FORGIVE! I FORGIVE! I FORGIVE! I FORGIVE! I FORGIVE!
  I FORGIVE! I FORGIVE! I FORGIVE! I FORGIVE!
I FORGIVE! I FORGIVE! I FORGIVE! I FORGIVE! I FORGIVE!
  I FORGIVE! I FORGIVE! I FORGIVE! I FORGIVE!
I FORGIVE! I FORGIVE! I FORGIVE! I FORGIVE! I FORGIVE!
  I FORGIVE! I FORGIVE! I FORGIVE! I FORGIVE!
I FORGIVE! I FORGIVE! I FORGIVE! I FORGIVE! I FORGIVE!
  I FORGIVE! I FORGIVE! I FORGIVE! I FORGIVE!
I FORGIVE! I FORGIVE! I FORGIVE! I FORGIVE! I FORGIVE!
  I FORGIVE! I FORGIVE! I FORGIVE! I FORGIVE!
I FORGIVE! I FORGIVE! I FORGIVE! I FORGIVE! I FORGIVE!
  I FORGIVE! I FORGIVE! I FORGIVE! I FORGIVE!
I FORGIVE! I FORGIVE! I FORGIVE! I FORGIVE! I FORGIVE!
  I FORGIVE! I FORGIVE! I FORGIVE! I FORGIVE!

I RELEASE ALL ANGER! I RELEASE ALL SHAME!
I RELEASE ALL BITTERNESS! I RELEASE ALL BLAME!
I RELEASE ALL ANGER! I RELEASE ALL SHAME!
I RELEASE ALL BITTERNESS! I RELEASE ALL BLAME!
I RELEASE ALL ANGER! I RELEASE ALL SHAME!
I RELEASE ALL BITTERNESS! I RELEASE ALL BLAME!
I RELEASE ALL ANGER! I RELEASE ALL SHAME!
I RELEASE ALL BITTERNESS! I RELEASE ALL BLAME!
I RELEASE ALL ANGER! I RELEASE ALL SHAME!
I RELEASE ALL BITTERNESS! I RELEASE ALL BLAME!
I RELEASE ALL ANGER! I RELEASE ALL SHAME!
I RELEASE ALL BITTERNESS! I RELEASE ALL BLAME!
I RELEASE ALL ANGER! I RELEASE ALL SHAME!
I RELEASE ALL BITTERNESS! I RELEASE ALL BLAME!
I RELEASE ALL ANGER! I RELEASE ALL SHAME!
I RELEASE ALL BITTERNESS! I RELEASE ALL BLAME!
I RELEASE ALL ANGER! I RELEASE ALL SHAME!
I RELEASE ALL BITTERNESS! I RELEASE ALL BLAME!
I RELEASE ALL ANGER! I RELEASE ALL SHAME!
I RELEASE ALL BITTERNESS! I RELEASE ALL BLAME!
I RELEASE ALL ANGER! I RELEASE ALL SHAME!
I RELEASE ALL BITTERNESS! I RELEASE ALL BLAME!
I RELEASE ALL ANGER! I RELEASE ALL SHAME!
I RELEASE ALL BITTERNESS! I RELEASE ALL BLAME!
I RELEASE ALL ANGER! I RELEASE ALL SHAME!
I RELEASE ALL BITTERNESS! I RELEASE ALL BLAME!
I RELEASE ALL ANGER! I RELEASE ALL SHAME!
I RELEASE ALL BITTERNESS! I RELEASE ALL BLAME!
I RELEASE ALL ANGER! I RELEASE ALL SHAME!
I RELEASE ALL BITTERNESS! I RELEASE ALL BLAME!
I RELEASE ALL ANGER! I RELEASE ALL SHAME!
I RELEASE ALL BITTERNESS! I RELEASE ALL BLAME!
I RELEASE ALL ANGER! I RELEASE ALL SHAME!
I RELEASE ALL BITTERNESS! I RELEASE ALL BLAME!

I AM FREE!

Books by Holly Roberts Merrell...

To learn more about the author and more in depth detail of her personal experiences regarding her books, please visit hollyrobertsmerrell.com.

www.ingramcontent.com/pod-product-compliance
Lightning Source LLC
Chambersburg PA
CBHW041818040426
42452CB00001B/14